Positive About Inspection

Positive About Inspection

Mike Tilling
and
Paul Nash

Routledge
Taylor & Francis Group

LONDON AND NEW YORK

First published 2000 by Gower Publishing

Reissued 2018 by Routledge
2 Park Square, Milton Park, Abingdon, Oxon OX14 4RN
711 Third Avenue, New York, NY 10017, USA

Routledge is an imprint of the Taylor & Francis Group, an informa business

Publisher's Note
The publisher has gone to great lengths to ensure the quality of this reprint but points out that some imperfections in the original copies may be apparent.

Disclaimer
The publisher has made every effort to trace copyright holders and welcomes correspondence from those they have been unable to contact.

Typeset in Plantin Light

ISBN 13: 978-1-138-72526-3 (hbk)
ISBN 13: 978-1-315-19197-3 (ebk)

Contents

The material in *Positive About Inspection* should be read in conjunction with the publications of the Training Standards Council and the companion volume *Standards-based Training and Development*, also by Mike Tilling and Paul Nash (published by Gower Publishing Limited).

Acknowledgements

We would like to thank all those who have been so generous in giving their time in helping with the preparation of this manual. Any omissions or errors in the text are entirely the responsibility of the authors.

In particular we thank the following:

From the Training Standards Council:
David Sherlock and Helen Peggs
and inspectors from the expert
reading group:
Colin Ashton
Matthew Coffey
Lesley Davies
John Grimmer
Philip Howard
Barbara Hughes
Jane Riddell
Jane Robinson

From York Business College:
Margaret Taylor
From City Centre Training
(Northern) Ltd:
John Weir
Annie Weir
Keith Tweddle
Jackie Adams and the Business
Admin. team
Tanya deQuincey and all the team
in Cumbria
From York Consulting Ltd:
Jo Cutter
From Access Training Ltd:
Julie Reay

Chapter 1

Introduction

The publication of *Raising the Standard* in 1998 established, for the first time, a rigorous framework for judging the quality of provision delivered by organisations responsible for government-funded training programmes. In addition, the framework is designed to enhance public confidence in government-funded training and promote a number of desirable outcomes, such as the achievement of national training targets and lifelong learning.

The Training Standards Council is responsible for overseeing the development and maintenance of the self-assessment and inspection framework, and acts as the guardian of the standards. The Council is an independent body and complements other organisations which have responsibility for inspecting provision in schools, colleges and higher education.

Training providers will be inspected once during each four-year cycle. The inspections will be led by a full-time inspector supported by a team of associate inspectors who will each take responsibility for one occupational area. If the number of trainees in an occupational area is large, there may be more than one associate inspector allocated. In addition, associate inspectors will be nominated to deal with each of the four generic aspects, although all inspectors will be expected to contribute to them. The lead inspector may inspect an occupational area and will do some of the generic aspects. There is no hard and fast rule specifying the role of lead inspectors, but they will inspect some aspect of provision, unless the inspection is very large.

Raising the Standard considers training under seven aspects of provision. The three for each occupational area are:

• training and assessment
• trainees' achievements
• resources.

The four generic aspects are:

• equal opportunities
• trainer support
• management of training
• quality assurance.

The inclusion of equal opportunities as a generic aspect is currently a unique feature of the Council's inspections and reflects the importance attached to it by the government. Work-based learning is viewed as the last safety net for some people and a final opportunity to acquire the skills needed to secure a job.

The detection of fraud is one aspect of the Council's work, though by far the greater proportion of inspection time is spent examining the legitimate work of reputable organisations.

Positive About Inspection is concerned with self-assessment and offers guidance on how to respond to development needs identified as part of that process. This book, in considering the process of inspection, complements, and is a companion volume to, *Standards-based Training and Development*. It considers the process of inspection. The two are quite clearly linked, but only those providers with government-funded training contracts will be subjected to inspection once every four years. Other providers will want to use only the self-assessment and development materials in *Standards-based Training and Development*.

This book approaches inspection using two distinct perspectives. The first of these is a linear account of an inspection presented through the 'journal' entries of an inspector and a trainer working in an organisation undergoing inspection. The 'Provider's commentary' and the 'Inspector's commentary' are fictionalised accounts, but based on observations made by trainers and inspectors in the course of an inspection. There is a space for you to comment on the diary entries as they unfold.

The second element is a description of ten typical encounters which may occur in the course of an inspection. Each encounter is analysed from the point of view of what the inspector wants to get out of it, and adds some typical questions which may be asked. The encounters attempt to reflect the detailed nature of the inspection process.

Chapter 2

Preparing for inspection

When asked what inspectors will be examining, one recently inspected training provider replied, 'If you do it, they'll inspect it'. The inspection process is exceptionally thorough and those providers who have been through it have been astonished by the detailed examination of every aspect of their provision. The process is, without doubt, intensive and disruptive, but also highly informative and useful. The criticisms the inspectors make may be compared to depth charges which force the submarines of strength and weakness to the surface. You may have always known they were there, but now you have to deal with them.

Inspection teams have to process a great deal of information in a short space of time. However, they are specialists in their fields: they know the subject, the systems and how to judge the quality of provision. Their presence on your premises gives you an opportunity to look with a fresh pair of eyes at what you do: you may be too close to be objective.

The inspectors will expect to construct the report on your organisation, as the inspection progresses, and complete it within ten days. If you have a number of sites, inspectors will need to keep each other informed, probably by fax and telephone, so that the report is consistent. The report will be published on the Training Standard Council's website within ten weeks, following rigorous editing.

You can expect that inspectors will probe until they are satisfied that they are clear about the nature of your provision. The daily feedback process is therefore essential, not just for providers so that they can present themselves in a better light, but also for the inspectors so that they can raise issues openly and work towards a 'no surprises' feedback on the last day.

The format of the feedback sessions is carefully constructed. It takes the form of a discussion between inspectors to which providers are invited to offer more evidence and clarify any of the issues. Inspectors will enumerate the 'emerging issues' which will then be discussed with the nominee and may be written up on a flipchart. The provider's representatives are encouraged to produce further evidence, but this will have to be convincing if minds are to be changed. What begins to emerge as a strength or weakness in the first few days may have disappeared by the end of the process.

Inspectors want to see good practice and they will work hard to uncover it. Unfortunately, many providers only hear the negative criticisms and tend to ignore the strengths. This is understandable, but it does contribute to feelings of anxiety. Inspectors will try to be constructive, although they will not offer advice about how to remedy any of the weaknesses they uncover. They will, however, ensure that providers are not criticised twice for the same weakness – that is, a weakness will not appear against an occupational area as well as a generic aspect.

You may find that some inspectors present information in a way that does not suit you. This is unfortunate, but, at all costs, avoid taking criticism personally; feelings of resentment will inhibit the extent to which you can learn from the experience.

STOP AND THINK

How well do you accept praise? Or deal with criticism?
How can you comment on 'emerging issues' in a way that is constructive rather than defensive?

You will be faced with the issues of praise and criticism during an inspection. Perhaps the first step you could take is to consider who will be attending the meetings – how will they react when weaknesses begin to emerge in their own area? How well do they accept praise?

The role of the lead inspector will vary with the size of the organisation being inspected. The smaller the organisation, the more likely it is that the lead will be directly involved in inspecting provision themselves. With a larger inspection, the lead will probably be engaged in staff interviews, checking the growing body of evidence and following up on issues raised by assistant inspectors.

As the inspection progresses, a number of charts may appear on the walls. Such charts will set out the totals seen of:

- employers visited and interviewed
- trainees interviewed
- portfolios examined
- observations of training sessions
- assessments observed
- trainee reviews
- staff interviewed.

Since they are available for anyone to review, the charts contribute to the openness of the process and they also provide a visual representation of the progress of the inspection. However, they may only be necessary on larger inspections.

As the inspection gets under way, inspectors will be looking for trainers who know and understand the overall aims of the company. They will expect the organisation to have inducted staff thoroughly and made an effort to acquaint everyone with the mission statement. They will not demand uniformity, but they will expect some consistency in: positive staff attitudes to trainees and employers; the active promotion of equal opportunities and other policies; and agreement on completing paperwork. An inspection is the ideal opportunity for you to verify whether these are characteristics of your organisation.

Reports published by the Training Standards Council indicate that the most common weaknesses are:

- poor links between on- and off-the-job training
- a lack of employer involvement (especially in reviewing trainee progress)
- inadequate subcontractor monitoring
- poor initial assessment
- key skills not integrated with vocational training
- inadequate assessment of prior learning (APL)
- no records of trainee support
- lack of detail in training plans
- limited use of training plans
- inadequate management information systems.

While it would be a mistake to concentrate on weakness, these areas of concern do suggest a starting point when considering where to direct your energies in the first pass of self-assessment.

Do not neglect the basics in preparation for the inspection. Check the time of year that your inspection falls due. For example, if it is in February/March it is likely that you will be preoccupied with fulfilling contracts. An inspection falling in the winter months may mean that you will have to prepare for a higher level of absenteeism, on the part of both staff and students, from illness. Make sure that the toilets are supplied with soap and towels. Photocopy *Raising the Standard* and arrange for it to be placed on all staff noticeboards. Identify a reasonably large, well-lit room which the inspection team can use as a base. Ensure that everyone is thoroughly briefed about where they have to be, the times that they should be there and where they will be taking their inspector. Inspections run to a very tight timetable, and any failures will reflect badly on your capacity to organise in general.

STOP AND THINK

What 'housekeeping' factors will you have to bear in mind for your inspection? For example, which room would you use for the final day? If the inspection calls for a large team, and they want to prepare documents on the spot, does the room contain enough power points for their laptop computers?

Chapter 3

The role of the nominee

Think very carefully about who is to act as your inspection nominee. They should:

- be knowledgeable about all aspects of the organisation's work
- have the authority to direct staff to undertake tasks specific to the inspection
- be capable of dealing with criticism and accepting praise gracefully
- be assertive under examination by people who are experts in their field.

Before the inspection begins, nominees will attend a conference where they can meet inspectors and representatives of other providers about to be inspected. This conference will give detailed information about the background to the Training Standards Council, the scope of inspection and the process itself. Nominees will have the opportunity to ask questions about any details that concern them, both in open sessions and in small groups. To get the most out of the conference, nominees should:

- consult widely about the concerns of staff and carry them forward as questions to be answered
- read as much as possible about inspection, including a selection of reports on other organisations
- collect all the handouts from the conference and edit them into an internal publication which is circulated to all teams, with a commentary.

The nominee will have their normal work to do during the inspection but, for this period only (once every four years), they must work around the inspection. The nominee must exercise foresight in predicting the paperwork that inspectors will want to see and view the whole process as a marathon, not a sprint: your organisation must be as smooth and efficient on the last day as it is on the first. If at all possible, the nominee should be released from all other duties for the period of the inspection.

One of the nominee's principal tasks is to organise the visits to trainees. The timetable for visits must minimise travel and other wasted time. If the start of a day is disrupted or delayed, inspectors will see this as a lack of organisation. There may be a perfectly genuine reason for the problem, but inspectors know that such disruptions are sometimes delaying tactics. Whatever the reason, the inspectors may see the organisation as either disorganised or devious – neither of which is desirable.

STOP AND THINK

Who is the right person to act as nominee for your organisation? There may be only one possibility for you, particularly if you are a small provider. On the other hand, you may want to use this as a staff development opportunity.

Chapter 4

The inspection experience

While inspectors are on your premises, they are always on duty. They are unlikely to stop for lunch, usually preferring to take a sandwich while they work. They may appear distant and brisk in their dealings with you. For example, their code of practice does not allow them to accept anything but the minimum amount of hospitality (for example, morning coffee), but this businesslike attitude is the result of their desire to complete the inspection in the time available. Some inspectors may have met before, but generally the team assembled to inspect your organisation will be unique.

They may want to take the opportunity of discussing aspects of an adviser's/ assessor's work as they drive from one site to another, although they should always ask the driver's permission. Staff are entitled to refuse such discussion if they prefer to concentrate on their driving and controlling any nerves. One training adviser was so nervous at having an inspector in her car that she was visibly shaking as she engaged first gear. The inspector warned her just in time that she was driving on the wrong side of the road!

THE FIRST BRIEFING MEETING

For inspectors, the first day will begin with an opportunity to meet new and old colleagues, and for the distribution of last-minute information. The lead inspector will remind associate inspectors of their professional responsibilities before going on to the provider's premises.

The official business begins with a meeting at the training provider's site. A representative of the training provider, probably the managing director, will already have been invited to make some opening remarks, but not all choose to do so. The main purpose of this meeting is to launch the process and offer an opportunity for inspectors and key personnel to meet and begin to build a relationship. The briefing may consist of the history, geographical 'catchment area', main contracts, SOC areas and other work of the organisation. However, the presentation should not duplicate information which is already available in the self-assessment report.

JOURNAL ENTRIES

Provider's commentary	Notes/comments

Monday, 9.00 a.m.

Until this morning, when our car park suddenly swarmed with five cars bearing eight inspectors, it had all seemed a little unreal. We had worked our way through quite a successful self-assessment report, then the nominee conference, the visit by the lead inspector and the form filling, but we couldn't bring ourselves to believe that it was actually going to happen to us.

I gulped the last of my coffee, tucked the overheads under my arm and headed for reception . . .

Inspector's commentary

Monday, 8.15 a.m.

Brief meeting in the hotel before we set off for the provider's premises. I knew most of the other inspectors, but I had not met two of them before. We spent a little time checking that we had the correct documentation with us (some forms have recently been revised) and shared impressions of the self-assessment report.

Once the preliminaries are over, there is a need to check schedules and ensure that no problems have arisen which will require a change of plan. The schedule of observations, interviews and visits is carefully worked out to give a representative picture of the organisation and any disruption will require an appropriately flexible response from the provider.

JOURNAL ENTRIES

Provider's commentary	Notes/comments

Monday, 9.45 a.m.

I thought my introduction went quite well – considering. Managed to keep our history, geography, student profile and TEC contract summary down to less than ten minutes (not the five I had promised Adele, my PA), and I think that joke about Yorkshiremen went down quite well, although halfway through I was suddenly aware that it might have an effect on our equal opportunities rating – too late now.

Provider's commentary (*contd.*)	Notes/comments (*contd.*)

Provider's commentary (*contd.*)

We were introduced to all the inspectors. They smiled and looked us straight in the eye. At 9.25 I got the nod that all our staff who were accompanying the inspectors were waiting in reception. At least the start of day one has gone smoothly.

Inspector's commentary

Monday, 9.30 a.m.

This is a fairly large inspection. I don't like descending *en masse* at 9.00 a.m., but I can't see any other way of doing it.

The introduction to the organisation was OK: it only lasted fifteen minutes and did not repeat too much of the information we already had. His joke about Yorkshiremen suggests that they have at least retained their sense of humour, although I wonder if he knows that the lead inspector is from Sheffield.

Notes/comments (*contd.*)

OBSERVING A TRAINING SESSION

There may not be many opportunities for inspectors to observe trainers teaching a group of trainees, since a large proportion of the learning will be work-based. However, for those sessions that they do see, they will have a clear vision of what makes successful classroom practice. Much of the quality of provision in this area we take for granted, and inspectors will be no exception. However, they will be surprised, and are likely to comment adversely, if they observe:

- poor-quality learning materials and aids (for example, third-generation photocopied handouts, an overhead projector that does not work)
- a trainer using inappropriate language (for example, too technical, too impersonal)
- inadequate learning environment (for example, no wall displays, shoddy furniture, poorly maintained accommodation)
- evidence of a lack of planning (for example, no explicit objectives for the session, subject matter presented illogically, no observable conclusion)
- poor relationships with trainees (for example, not knowing their names, use of sarcasm, patronising attitudes)
- poor technique (no opportunities for the trainees to contribute, lack of pace, no adaptation of process to content, no link made to work-based practice)

Inspectors will use a standard observation form to record their comments on the session. After a session, they may ask the trainer:

- What was the purpose of this session?
- Do you always use the board that much? Do you think that your candidates are capable of making notes and listening to you simultaneously?
- Were you aware that the same individual answered all your questions?

- Can I see the training plans for these candidates?
- Can I see their portfolios?
- Why did you choose to ask them to work in pairs/individually/in groups?
- Whose work is this on the wall? When was it last changed?
- How good are your attendance rates? Show me the register.
- What was your pass rate for the previous group? How are your current candidates progressing?
- Do you have any trainees in this group with special needs? How are their needs being met? Have they progressed as quickly as you would expect?

Inspectors will almost certainly want to talk to members of the group. All inspectors have considerable experience of training and trainees, and will spend some time putting them at ease and explaining what an inspection is all about. They will emphasise that it is the organisation, not the trainees, that is the subject of inspection.

JOURNAL ENTRIES

Provider's commentary	Notes/comments

Provider's commentary

Monday, 9.50 a.m.

First hitch: our coordinator for Motor Vehicle has broken down on the motorway. He was due to be interviewed at 10.00 a.m. – I'll have to find an alternative. Perhaps I could substitute an interview with our placements manager, Janice. She won't be pleased, but at least we can demonstrate some flexibility as an organisation and we are strong in this area. Not sure what else Janice is doing – I'll check, if I have the time.

Inspector's commentary

Monday, 2.00 p.m.

So far so good. The trainees I have spoken to are friendly, open and cooperative. They like their trainers. My visits have been well organised and the employers have been knowledgeable about NVQs and work-based learning. However, spotted that two of them had no equal opportunities policy – this will go back to the inspector reporting on EO as a generic aspect.

DAILY FEEDBACK

At the end of each day, the inspection team will meet with the nominee and other representatives of the provider to discuss their findings. The inspectors will place great emphasis on the provisional nature of their observations in the early stages and will talk about 'emerging issues', rather than strengths and weaknesses. Providers can signal their disagreement at any point and produce evidence to refute the inspector's conclusions. For example, inspectors may criticise the way in which interim reviewing of candidates is carried out because the documents they have seen make only brief or single-word summaries. In such situations, the provider may be able to produce evidence which shows that other trainers have been much more comprehensive in their reports. However, criticism may then shift to quality assurance, since the design of the document seems to offer only limited space for advisers to comment.

Feedback at the end of the first day will consider the emerging issues that inspectors have observed in the occupational areas. Comment on the generic areas will not normally appear until day two. Issues will either remain current or be crossed off the flipchart if they are resolved to the inspector's satisfaction.

Grades will never be discussed with the training provider until the grading meeting. Providers should not assume that an apparent numerical superiority of positives rather than negatives will necessarily mean a Grade 3 or above. The important consideration is the impact on the learning experience of the trainee, and this may not be reflected in the number of positive or negative issues.

JOURNAL ENTRIES

Provider's commentary	Notes/comments
Monday, 5.30 p.m.	
Feedback at the end of the first day: inspectors picked up on a weakness in work placements in two occupational areas! Can't believe it. If this is a weakness, what are the other aspects going to be like? They said something about strengths in quality of training and induction, but I can't recall much about that. To be honest, I was in a bit of a daze, what with all this going on and normal business to conduct. And this is just day one!	
Inspector's commentary	
Monday, 5.30 p.m.	
Well, they were a bit surprised by my comments on induction and recording trainees' progress. As usual, we talked about 'emerging issues' and they asked us about 'weaknesses'. I think it says something about our culture that providers concentrate on the weaknesses and barely hear what we say about their stronger points. My impression is that they have taken the message about being open and honest to heart.	

MEETINGS WITH TRAINEES AT THE PROVIDER'S PREMISES

Inspectors will normally expect to sample a percentage of trainees in each occupational area, though there is no precise regulation as to how many they should see. The percentage may be 50 per cent in a smaller provider, although only 30 per cent may be possible with a medium-sized organisation. However, their schedule for accomplishing this is very tight. They will expect to meet with trainees individually to probe their perceptions and then, if possible, see others as a group to widen discussion. They will probably begin by explaining who they are and what they are trying to do.

Inspectors will be checking whether trainers know and understand the needs of their trainees. They will probe for candidate's understanding of their training programme, whether it is a Modern Apprenticeship, National Traineeship or any other government programme, and how well they understand NVQs. They will look at portfolios and other documentation.

Although they may be fiercely loyal to their training providers, trainees will tell the truth about what they have experienced no matter how a provider may try to influence them otherwise. If a provider wants them to say the right thing, then the provider must do the right thing.

Inspectors may ask trainees:

- What programme are you on/level are you at?
- Have NVQs been explained to you?
- Do you understand how you will be assessed?
- When were you given this information (was it just before the inspection began)?
- Tell me about how you started on this programme.
- Take me through a typical day at the training centre.
- Do you think you are on the right course, at the right level?
- How were you assessed when you arrived?
- How was health and safety explained to you?
- What progress have you made to date?
- What kind of initial assessment did you have?
- What was your involvement in constructing your individual training plan/ assessment plan?
- What work have you gathered for your portfolio?
- Can you explain this aspect of your portfolio?
- Have you done anything for key skills?
- Do you have a workbook to help with what you have to learn?
- Do you know about the equal opportunities policy?
- I see from your records that you are visually impaired. What has been done to make sure that you get full access to everything you need?
- When do you expect to finish your course? Will you finish by your target date?
- What do you expect to do next? Have your options been explained to you?
- How often do you see your assessor? What happens? Has the same person been your assessor all the time or have they changed?

JOURNAL ENTRIES

Provider's commentary	Notes/comments

Provider's commentary

Tuesday, 10.00 a.m.

Comments coming in from our staff indicate that inspectors' questions were searching and that they were tenacious in pursuing the information they wanted. Inquiries seem to range from why an assessment form had not been signed to the trainer's view of the needs of local industry.

Got a complaint from Janice that she had seen three inspectors yesterday when she was only expecting one. Apart from the interview substituting for Motor Vehicle, it turns out that the deputy manager had referred an inspector directly to her without consulting anyone. Janice said she had tried to 'wing it' (her phrase) but she just did not really have the information at her fingertips for Retail and Care. Told her to get it sorted and report to the lead inspector by lunchtime. What was it she was saying as she put the phone down?

Inspector's commentary

Tuesday, 10.30 a.m.

What was I saying about being open? One trainer claimed that her retention rate was 'high' when in fact the statistics showed that it was no better than average for the organisation. What she had failed to register was how good her achievement rate for NVQs was. I pointed this out and suggested that I should record this as a strength. She saw the sense of my suggestion.

Documents check revealed that a number of assessments had not been signed, although internal verification in general seems to be very thorough.

WORK-BASED MEETINGS WITH TRAINEES

The context for this type of meeting may be a trainee support visit or an observation of an assessment in progress. Inspectors are looking for on-site meetings to be conducted in an orderly manner and in a way that supports the achievements of the trainee. Assessors may be tempted to interview a trainee just for the purposes of showing an inspector what goes on. However, they should exercise judgement and avoid trying to interview while a trainee is engaged in performing a work task. For example, one inspector observed an assessor attempting to interview a trainee in a supermarket while she was working on the checkout and trying to deal with customers.

Some workplaces are easier to conduct meetings in than others. Many will take place in staff tearooms or possibly in a vacant office with minimal comforts. The inspectors will be looking for trainers who can overcome such limitations.

They may ask the trainer:

- What was the purpose of that meeting? Assessment? Advice? Learning support?
- How often do you visit candidates?
- Do all candidates receive the same kind of treatment?
- How do you strike a balance between recording your findings and keeping the assessment flowing?
- When do you use open/closed questions?
- How do you deal with assessing a unit if you are not fully conversant with it?
- How do you respond when trainees have not done the work they agreed to?
- Do you think you are on a paper chase or engaged in a genuine training and development process?
- Who sets the targets?

They may ask the trainee very similar questions to cross-check the trainer's perceptions. For example:

- What was the purpose of that meeting? Assessment? Advice? Learning support?
- Do you think all candidates receive the same kind of treatment?
- What happens when you have not done the work you agreed to?
- Who sets the targets?
- How often does your assessor visit? What happens?
- How often and where do you do off-the-job training?
- Do you discuss the training course back at work? Does your work-based supervisor know and understand what your course is all about? Does your trainer know about and understand what happens in your workplace?
- Do you like attending the training centre?
- What kind of support do you get from people at work?
- Have you done anything for key skills?
- Do you understand why you have to do the tasks that are set?
- How many units have you had signed off?
- What is your next step when you have finished this programme?
- How was health and safety explained to you?

JOURNAL ENTRIES

Provider's commentary	Notes/comments
Tuesday, 5.30 p.m. End of day two, and I think I'm going mad. We identified 11 strengths in Business Admin. on our self-assessment report. The inspector rejected them all as standard	

practice, but then found four strengths we had not recognised. At least something good has come out of that.

I'm suicidal about Construction, though. The number of weaknesses has gone up to five while strengths have gone down to two. The problems are:

- individual training needs not systematically identified
- poor trainee understanding of NVQs
- trainees unclear about what to do after reviews
- insufficient on-the-job assessments
- poor coordination of on- and off-the-job training.

Have we got any evidence to demonstrate that these are not accurate observations? We received our first feedback on the generic areas. We seem to have an emerging strength in trainee support, with the others at the 'satisfactory' level – as far as we can tell.

Inspector's commentary

Tuesday, 4.00 p.m.

Saw a very good training session and checked some portfolios. They were individual and reflected the personalities of the candidates. I also liked the use they had made of wall displays, particularly the one showing appropriate dress for different work situations. Some of the candidates could be making quicker progress, but they seem content. I will feed this back to the trainer concerned and discuss it with other inspectors, but I don't think it will be appearing in tonight's feedback.

Tuesday, 9.00 p.m.

Managed to get my report writing up-to-date.

COMPANY LINKS

One of the issues raised most frequently in inspection reports is that of the link between on- and off-the-job training. Inspectors recognise that providers face problems with some employers who are reluctant to lose the trainee's productivity for one day a week; make constant demands to fit training into work schedules without reciprocating with flexibility themselves; and have premises which are not conducive to learning. Having recognised these difficulties, the inspectors will be concerned to see how they are overcome. They want to know what is being done to train and support the individual in the workplace and how employers are being engaged in the process.

They may ask an employer:

- Are you clear about the qualifications your trainee is pursuing?
- Have you seen the trainee's training plan and their assessment plan?
- Do you have your own equal opportunities policy? And/or are you aware of the training providers equal opportunities policy?
- Are you clear about the standards trainees are expected to achieve?
- How many trainees have you had with this training company?
- Have you changed providers? If so, why?
- If you point out a problem with a training programme, does anything happen?
- What type and amount of support do you receive from the provider? How many site visits do trainees receive? Is it enough?
- Are you happy with the support you receive from the training provider? Do you discuss the programme with them?
- Do you have any comment to make on the quality of the trainees you receive?
- How do you find out from your trainees what has happened during review sessions and off-the-job training?

JOURNAL ENTRIES

Provider's commentary	Notes/comments
Wednesday, 10.00 a.m. We have now given amended information about work placements to the lead inspector, and we are doing what we can for Construction. I tried to get some feel for emerging grades from him – nothing doing. Not much sleep last night. This is turning out to be much harder than I had expected. **Inspector's commentary** *Wednesday, 9.45 a.m.* The person allocated to take me to see trainees and employers has not turned up. I took the opportunity to review some quality issues while I was in their head office. I was particularly interested in their documentation for reviewing progress. The layout of the document seems to restrict comment to a single word and a signature. Unfortunately, the files were not where they should have been. There was embarrassment all round when they turned up in the conference room	

Provider's commentary (*contd.*)	Notes/comments (*contd.*)
where the lead inspector was doing some checking himself.	
Heard some harsh words from the manager when my guide finally arrived. He had gone to the wrong office.	

STAFF INTERVIEW: GENERAL

Inspectors want to know what actually happens in a training organisation. They will not be impressed by fine words or expressions of loyalty to trainees and employers. They want to know what it is that you do to fulfil the written and unwritten bargain between trainer and trainee. A likely starting point for interviews is the trainer's job description. They know that, without explicitly allocated responsibilities, jobs do not get done. They will probe to uncover the relative priorities staff give to their functions and whether some of them are omitted completely because of a lack of time.

Inspectors will not ask all staff the same questions, so it is not possible to prepare a checklist. However, they will be looking for a thorough understanding of the job role; appropriate qualifications and experience; staff development that really makes a difference to the quality of training; the quality of the relationships with trainees and employers; and how staff liaise with one another.

They may ask:

- What is your role?
- How long have you done this? What is your background?
- What do you feel about working here?
- Who are you responsible to? What are you responsible for?
- How does the company carry out the internal verification (IV) process?
- Why is there so much written material in their portfolios? Would other kinds of evidence have done as well?
- How is feedback given and recorded?
- How is sampling carried out?
- Where are appropriate documents kept?
- What meetings do you attend? Do they achieve their aims?
- What is the purpose of on-site visits? How often do they occur?
- How do you deal with complaints?
- What staff development have you had? Did it meet your/the organisation's needs?
- How do you meet the specific needs of disabled people?
- Is the number of trainees you support manageable?
- Does the organisation's documentation help or hinder your work?

STAFF INTERVIEW: FOR A SPECIFIC PURPOSE

Inspectors will want to discuss policy issues and probe their detailed implementation with staff who have specific responsibilities. They will not be making any judgements about the procedures in the abstract, only considering whether they work for the organisation concerned. In discussion, inspectors will investigate how the systems work, and they will continue to question until the processes are fully explained.

Inspectors will almost certainly spend considerable time with the person responsible for quality assurance. They will want to know how training is evaluated and how achievement targets are set. They will search for evidence that systems exist and that they are being used. Inspectors will not expect to see a document to support every aspect of quality assurance, but they will expect to see some form of evidence that something is done when a situation demands it.

They may ask:

- What are your main responsibilities?
- How do you sample the opinions of trainees and employers? How do you use the information once it is gathered?
- Is your documentation standardised? Show me how it works.
- Does your documentation support all aspects of training?
- Do you have a quality assurance manual? Is it used?
- Do you have an example of an issue raised by a trainee, which was discussed and then acted upon?
- What are your local and national benchmarks for setting targets? How often do you evaluate progress towards achieving targets?
- How do you get to know about comments from external verifiers? How do you check that their recommendations have been implemented?

JOURNAL ENTRIES

Provider's commentary

Notes/comments

Wednesday, 5.00 p.m.

A clearer picture is now beginning to emerge. It does not take a genius to see that where weaknesses outnumber strengths, we may be in trouble. We have managed to get a number of weaknesses removed from occupational areas, but only because some of them are now seen as generic. This is particularly true of Quality Assurance where a failure to disseminate good practice disappeared from one area only to show up as an overall weakness for the organisation. I am a bit concerned that this may be reducing our argument about strengths in generic areas.

Inspector's commentary

Wednesday, 5.30 p.m.

A pattern is now beginning to emerge and many of my comments have been reflected in those of other inspectors. The general picture is of a good-quality organisation with faults that are mainly attributable to previous practices which have encouraged an emphasis on compliance and tick-boxes. What we have seen is an organisation which emphasises:

- trainee support which is verifiable through hard evidence on retention and achievement, not just its 'warm and friendly' feel
- better than average links with local employers
- quality assurance which makes an impact on training (despite no Investors in People or ISO 9000)
- good control of subcontracted work (although the problem experienced by many providers of coordinating on- and off-the-job training is present).

DOCUMENTS CHECK

Documents checking will be built into the inspection schedule, but an inspector may ask for a particular document at any time. They may also institute a documents check if time suddenly becomes available because of a cancelled meeting.

Inspectors are looking for correct figures and precise administrative procedures. They will want to reconcile the figures given on the pre-inspection pro-forma with what they find on-site. They will check to see whether documentation is clear, regularly completed and thorough. Organisations will be given every opportunity to explain anomalies and localised difficulties.

Of particular interest to inspectors are the records of internal and external verifiers. They may, for example, check to see if issues identified by an external verifier have been picked up and acted upon. Sometimes an inspector will identify issues missed by an external verifier. For example, one inspector found that an internal verifier was not occupationally competent when the Common Accord clearly states that they should be. There was no reference to this from the external verifier. Inspectors will not accept that a weakness can be explained by saying that external verifiers, or the TEC, were satisfied.

They may ask:

- Is each document up-to-date?
- Do the dates indicate that it was completed for the inspection?
- Are all appropriate documents signed? If not, why not?
- Is the member of staff responsible for the documentation able to explain any anomalies without excuses?
- Is the level of detail in documentation appropriate?

- Do trainees receive duplicate copies of documents?
- Do CVs reveal that staff are appropriately qualified and experienced? How recent was the experience?
- Does one area have an example of good practice? How is this being disseminated across the organisation?

JOURNAL ENTRIES

Provider's commentary

Thursday, 11.00 a.m.

Last day. They are all together in the conference room at the moment, putting together their final thoughts. Now I look at it, perhaps we aren't doing as badly as I had thought. On the first two days I just did not hear them when they said we had some strengths, all I could hear was weakness, weakness, weakness.

We go in later for the grading, and then meet with the TEC and Government Office late afternoon.

Inspector's commentary

Thursday, 11.30 a.m.

Despite working until midnight on my report, I was still not entirely satisfied. It took advice from the lead inspector and colleagues before achieving the accuracy of expression I was seeking.

As we debated the finer points of our feedback, I could see the looks of astonishment on the faces of the nominee and other managers. Talking to them later, they expressed amazement at the vigour of the debate and the detailed questioning of the wording. A typical example was one of mine where I suggested that: 'Managers still train, assess and verify' was a strength. There was agreement that it was a strength, but the dispute concerned the word 'still'. Eventually we substituted 'continue to', and moved on to other considerations.

Notes/comments

PROCEDURES FOR THE FINAL DAY OF INSPECTION

The final day generally conforms to the pattern set out on page 23.

Drafting reports

The associate inspectors may spend a considerable proportion of the final day preparing their reports and final feedback comments. Some lead inspectors like to edit and return material to associates as the morning progresses, but this may not always be possible. They will be looking for clarity and directness in style. There should be no jargon and no hidden messages. Checks will be made to ensure that strengths really are more than just standard practice. For example, 'good relationships with trainees' is to be expected. For this to emerge as a strength, there must be something outstanding about the provision. There may be vigorous debate within the team on issues such as these.

Grading meeting

This is the final presentation of strengths and weaknesses, and inspectors will take pains to ensure that providers fully understand the evidence that lies behind their conclusions. This is the part of the process which providers can influence, and it is very important to ensure that all the evidence has been taken into account. However, judgements and grades are totally in the hands of the inspectors, based entirely on the evidence they have seen.

As each inspector confirms their view of the organisation's strengths and weaknesses, there may be further debate, but by now there should be no surprises about what the inspection team have to say. The grades are proposed and agreed by the team.

Final feedback

Towards the end of the day, representatives of the provider, the TEC and Government Office will be invited in for the final feedback. Procedures for this meeting are laid down, but there may be some variation depending on the lead inspector's judgement. For example, some lead inspectors prefer to feed back to the full senior management team, as well as to the external observers. However, debate is not allowed in the final feedback, only requests for clarification of specific points from TEC or Government Office representatives.

The final act of the inspection is for the lead to give their perceptions of the way that the team has worked and how successful the process has been. Again, this may vary with the preferred style of the lead inspector.

JOURNAL ENTRIES

Provider's commentary	Notes/comments
Thursday, 5.00 p.m.	
Well, it's all over. Not too bad – mostly 'threes', and our 'twos' outnumber our 'fours' (just). Pity about Construction, because I still don't think that we are as weak as they suggested, but a key strength like	

'training linked to local industrial need' could not offset the weaknesses.

Neither the TEC nor the GO representatives made much comment except to clarify the wording of one issue.

Overall, it was a worthwhile experience. We were driven to look at the quality of what we deliver. The inspection unearthed things we didn't know we were good at, while some of our so-called strengths turned out to be just standard practice. The immediate challenge is to raise the morale of some staff and draw up our action plan. We must also thank those trainees whom inspectors described as 'animated' in their support of us and their trainers.

Inspector's commentary

Thursday, 4.30 p.m.

This is my 22nd inspection and they don't get any easier. It is a very intense, though relatively brief, relationship with the training provider. This provider, along with most others has been open and honest in dealing with us and demonstrated good practice in many areas, as well as weaknesses in others. My job is to focus on the quality of the learning experience for trainees, and I am still learning how to judge that. If I didn't feel that I was making a significant contribution to improving the quality of training, I wouldn't do it.

Once the inspection is over, the lead inspector will complete the draft report and refer it to the provider for the checking of factual accuracy. It is then sent to the Training Standards Council offices where it is edited and moderated. The report is checked for:

- style
- content
- consistency
- an appropriate balance between strengths and weaknesses, which accurately reflect the grade awarded.

If there is any dispute, the report will be reconsidered with the lead inspector.

The final publication of the report will occur within ten weeks of the end of the inspection. The provider has a further eight weeks to prepare an action plan which builds on the contents of the inspection report, although most will have taken action well before that.

REINSPECTION

Any provider who receives a grade 4 or 5 will be reinspected within a year (see *Reinspection*, Training Standards Council, 1999). Around 50 per cent of providers inspected have received at least one 4 or 5. If the grade is in an occupational area, this alone will be reinspected. A 4 or 5 in a generic aspect will mean an inspection which samples across the occupational areas to ensure that improvements have been made and that they have been experienced by trainees.

The reinspection process will follow similar procedures to a normal inspection.

Using the outcomes of inspection

The great temptation after an inspection is to 'breathe a sigh of relief'. This is a typical and very human reaction – perhaps a reflection of the resistance we frequently experience from trainees who are reluctant to 'reflect' on the learning experience. However, it should be resisted. Even though the actual report will not be available until several weeks after the inspection has finished, providers should consider immediately how they can begin to deal with some of the issues revealed.

Inevitably, the focus will be on remedying weaknesses – and some issues may require immediate attention – but, at some point, you should consider how you can build on the strengths. There may also be a need to lift the morale of staff in some areas who may feel that their work has been misunderstood or insufficiently appreciated.

In the period after the inspection:

- draw up a provisional action plan based on the issues that are unlikely to change in the final report
- discuss the plan with the TEC
- use the provisional report to set a number of clear and short-term targets for development and try to make something happen quite quickly
- integrate your short-term action plan with a more comprehensive one when the full report is published.

STOP AND THINK

- How can you use the nominee after the inspection has finished?
- How can you catch the wind following inspection to drive up standards in all areas? And/or how will you plan for the likely feeling of deflation after the inspection is over?
- How can you use the inspection experience to draw your team together?
- Devise your own plan for the immediate post-inspection period.

JOURNAL ENTRY

Provider's final commentary

Notes/comments

I'm no nearer being able to understand my feelings about inspection now that it's all over and I've had time to think about it. I fluctuate between thinking that it was a worthwhile experience that forced us to find evidence for our strengths and pinpoint our weaknesses, and then thinking that the outcomes did not really warrant all the time and effort that went into the process.

I think that we engaged in a high level of debate about our provision with some very professional people and we were forced to confront the weaknesses that we knew were there, but had really done little about. I would say to others going through the process that: it is here to stay, it is as inevitable now as a change of season, and that those who see the potential for organisational development are those likely to benefit most.

STOP AND THINK

Put yourself in the place of a Training Standards Council inspector. You are inspecting a fairly large provider over a period of four days. As the inspection progresses, you identify a number of emerging issues which you put directly to the staff involved and to the nominee. How would you respond if the answers you received were:

- 'Oh, I didn't know you were going to look at that.'
  Your response:

- 'Our TEC contract doesn't cover that.'
  Your response:

- 'We do not receive sufficient payment to cover that.'
  Your response:

- 'Our TEC/external verifier has never raised it.'
  Your response:

- 'You don't seem to understand what we are trying to achieve.'
  Your response:

- 'I didn't know that was happening.'
  Your response:

- 'If you were to come in three months' time, it would be OK.'
  Your response:

What can you do to avoid being forced to make excuses like these?

T - #0062 - 270225 - C0 - 297/210/3 [5] - CB - 9781138725263 - Gloss Lamination